SENSATIONAL SYDNEY

Stunning Panoramic Views

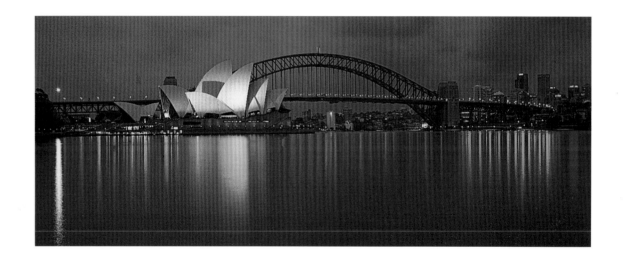

KEN DUNCAN

PANOGRAPHS®

Dominated by its famous Harbour Bridge and Opera House, Sydney is without doubt one of the most beautiful cities in the world. Golden beaches, sapphire seas and rivers that flow down from The Great Dividing Range into the city's sparkling bays, create a crown of natural beauty in which this jewel is set.

Harbour waters glistening in the sunlight like a million diamonds capture the city's essence of sparkling life. The great expanses of water that surround and run through Australia's major gateway provide a wonderful sense of freedom in the middle of its busy life. Brisk and dynamic, Sydney is rich in history and brimming with a vibrant cosmopolitan culture.

Blessed with a temperate climate, Sydney-siders just love outdoor entertainment. On an idyllic Sydney day the aromas of exquisite feasts being cooked on backyard barbeques waft through pockets of the city. Like the symphony of life it is, Sydney has many facets that all resonate with their own beauty, yet combine harmoniously in this sensational city of sun and fun.

TITLE PAGE
Sydney Opera House

LEFT
Avalon Beach

Ken Duncan was born in Mildura, Victoria, in 1954. A professional photographer since 1980, his work has received many industry awards both in Australia and overseas, and he is now recognized as one of the world's leading panoramic landscape specialists.

Typically casual about such accolades, Ken prefers to say he is just an average photographer with a mighty God. His goal and passion in life is simply to show people the beauty of God's creation, encouraging them to look beyond themselves to something far greater.

Enjoy the journey as you wander with Ken through the pages of this book, experiencing the wonder of an amazing city.

RIGHT
Splendour of Creation

PREVIOUS PAGE
Camp Cove & Watsons Bay

RIGHT
Archibald Fountain, Hyde Park

As day dawns, Sydney slowly shakes the slumber of the night. The harbour has had minimal traffic through the night and its mirrored surface reflects the glory of the coming day. Ferries are now beginning to scuttle around the harbour's fingered tributaries, drawing commuters into the heart of the bustling business areas, and the serene reflections will be broken in their wakes. The entrepreneur with his mobile breakfast stand capitalises on a captive audience. A man is silhouetted in the golden morning light as he paces at the end of the wharf, eagerly awaiting his ride to work. The ferry will come and life will go on, the timetables of man and of creation unaffected by our anxieties. We need to enjoy every moment as each new day has a multitude of possibilities for those who have eyes to see beyond their destination.

LEFT
Waiting for the ferry, Balmain

Shopping is definitely one of the best leisure activities one can engage in. I must admit that at first, being a guy, I was not a very good shopper. But my wife has helped me see the true value of retail therapy. Originally I considered shopping a chore. If its shirts we're after, we find a shop with shirts that fit, buy three or four in different colours and Voila! the shopping's done.

But there is far more to shopping. You have to take in the culture and be prepared to work an area, as you never know what little treasures may be hidden there. Patience is an important ingredient and you must not be single minded. You may have gone looking for a shirt but, if you remain open to possibilities, you could end up finding a cool gift that really reflects a good friend's personality.

Well, good luck with your shopping. With its wonderful cosmopolitan lifestyle Sydney has some of the most unique and diverse shopping available.

RIGHT
Strand Arcade

PREVIOUS PAGE
Bondi Beach

RIGHT
Macarthur's Homestead, Camden

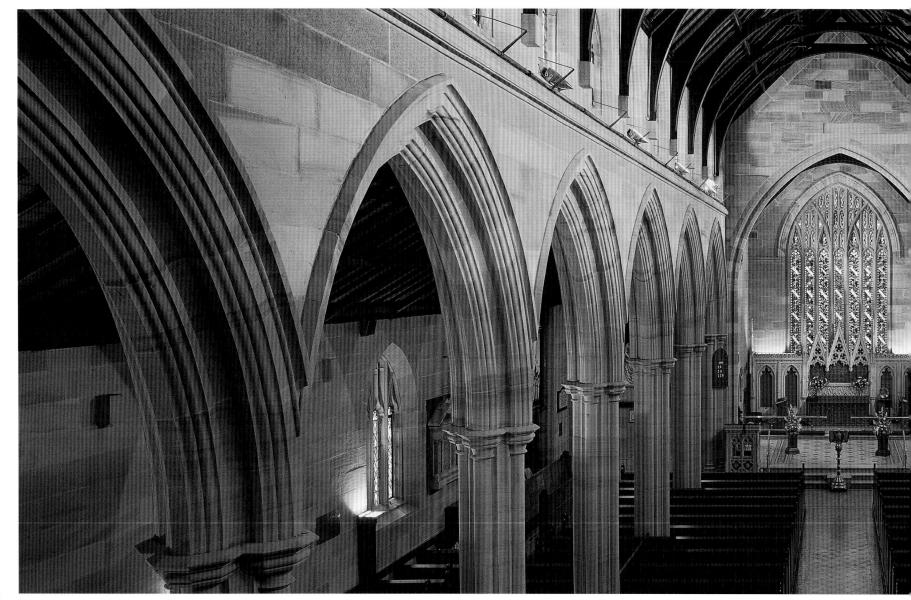

PREVIOUS PAGE
Sydney Aerial

LEFT
St Phillips Church

21

ABOVE
Clear waters, Palm Beach

ABOVE
Surfer girl, Palm Beach

It can certainly be said that Sydney was built on the rock as the abundant local sandstone was a highly favoured building material. Scattered throughout Sydney are some extraordinary edifices that beautifully portray the art of stone masonry and I am struck by the creativity and patience so evident in their creation.

When I look at buildings such as these pictured, and others like Saint Mary's Cathedral, I reflect on how proud the builders must have felt on their completion. The majesty and elegance of these masterpieces have far outlived those who poured their heart and soul into their creation.

I doubt that many of our modern structures will endure the test of time. Sydney Opera House leaps to mind, but how many more? It seems functionality, speed and cost have become the driving forces. I wonder, can we find the time to leave wonderful creative works for the future, or will our generation be known as the prefab concrete-jungle realists who lived on the bottom line.

PREVIOUS PAGE
Pastel sunrise, Freshwater Beach

LEFT
Sydney Town Hall and Queen Victoria Building

A stormy day. Warm and safe in my beachside cottage, I listened to waves breaking like thunderclaps, ghostly howling wind, the rush of rain. It seemed foolish to venture outside in such weather, but some urge beyond my understanding compelled me to go.

Soon the rain began to ease, and the clouds parted as though a great stone had been rolled aside, opening a doorway of pure light. This solitary fisherman stood baiting his hook while the clouds continued to boil and steam around him, as though at the very moment of creation.

If we prefer the comfort of shelter, we can miss many such opportunities for revelation and adventure.

RIGHT
Fisherman, Mona Vale Pool

PREVIOUS PAGE
Bondi from the air

ABOVE
Moreton Bay fig tree, Double Bay

ABOVE
Time to reflect, Manly Cove

NEXT PAGE
Sydney Opera House before dawn

Photography often involves a lot of waiting and I love to observe the many moods of Sydney's majestic beaches and sea pools. On this day, the swell was huge and the waves were coming in sets about ten minutes apart. Between these mammoth sets a few potential swimmers considered this an ideal spot for a swim. As people approached, I warned them of the lurking danger. After watching for a while, they thanked me and wisely turned back.

One couple, however, ignored my warning and continued on into the pool. Then, out on the horizon, a gigantic wall of water loomed. When these monster waves hit, the people were thrust into a wall of the pool then sucked towards the open sea. As the violent ocean threatened to smash them on the rocks, they managed to grab hold of a safety chain.

Battered and bruised, they climbed from the pool and humbly retreated, giving me a nod as they limped on by. It pays to be friendly to strangers, as we never know what important message they might share.

LEFT
Mahon Pool, Maroubra

There was not a single star twinkling through the pre-dawn sky as I waited at the beach in the dark and that usually means there won't be a great sunrise. It seemed hopeless, but I decided to wait and hope and see what the daylight would bring. This photograph just goes to prove that even in the midst of gloomy and turbulent times, light can break through to transform stormy circumstances into a spectacle of glory. Hope gives us strength to endure even when things seem out of control. If we do not stand, we will never know what wonders we may have missed.

RIGHT
Hope and Glory, Mona Vale

NEXT PAGE
Aerial view from Manly to the city

PREVIOUS PAGE
George Street, The Rocks

RIGHT
Sun seekers, Bronte Beach

LEFT
Sunrise reflections, Bayview

NEXT PAGE
Coogee Sea Pool

ABOVE
Old Pyrmont Bridge, Darling Harbour

ABOVE
Bennelong Point, Sydney Harbour

LEFT
Barrenjoey Lighthouse, Palm Beach

RIGHT
Shark Beach, Nielsen Park

NEXT PAGE
Parramatta River, Hunters Hill

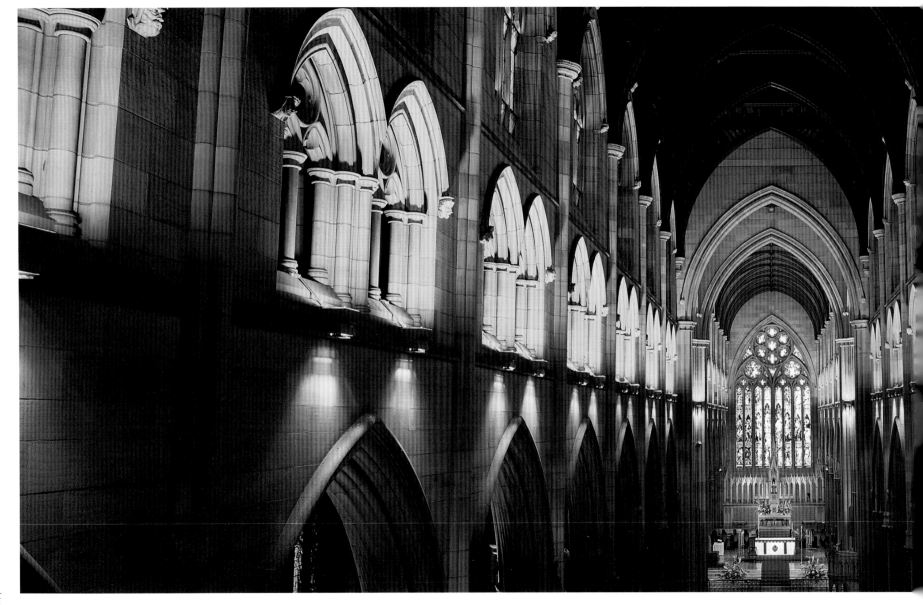

I love grand old churches. There is a presence about them — the result of all the prayers and praise of those who have come in search of divine direction. No matter how hard the human heart, when people enter sanctuaries such as these they can feel the closeness of God. Because I wanted to capture the ambience of St Mary's Cathedral in natural light, my exposures were long, and I spent many hours waiting and photographing. I saw many people from all walks of life visiting the Cathedral. Some came to marvel at the architecture, but most came seeking help or guidance. I was really touched by a young lady who was obviously very troubled. She wept silently, crying out from a hurting heart. When she left, it seemed as though she had found peace and renewed faith. I had a distinct sense that God had heard her prayers and assigned angels to watch over her.

LEFT
St Mary's Cathedral

The word Anzac was coined during the First World War — an acronym for the Australian and New Zealand Army Corps. Formed in December 1914, the Corps saw its first action on the Gallipoli Peninsula, Turkey, on April 25th, 1915. Over 10,000 Anzacs lost their lives in that campaign alone — one in every four soldiers who landed was killed. As bloody as the battle was, those who survived were then sent to the Western Front where the fighting was even worse. What an enormous price has been paid for our freedom! What do we do with this precious liberty for which so much blood was spilled? Do we take it for granted as we squabble over petty differences, or do we stand united for the future of our nation? There can never be too much recognition for the heroes who fought and died for our freedom. Hopefully this bridge, named in their honour, will be a constant reminder: *Lest We Forget.*

RIGHT
Anzac Bridge, sunset

PREVIOUS PAGE
Darling Harbour

ABOVE
Fort Denison, Sydney Harbour

ABOVE
Bare Island, Botany Bay

NEXT PAGE
Sydney Harbour Bridge Climb

LEFT
Taronga Park Zoo

RIGHT
Barrenjoey Head

ABOVE

New Year's Eve fireworks, Sydney Harbour

SENSATIONAL SYDNEY

*First published in 2002
by Ken Duncan Panographs®
Pty Limited
Panographs® is a registered
Trademark of Ken Duncan Australia
Wide Holdings Pty Ltd.
ABN 21 050 235 606
PO Box 3015, Wamberal
NSW 2260, Australia
Telephone +61 2 4367 6777
Email: panos@kenduncan.com*

*Copyright photography and text:
© Ken Duncan 2002
Designed by Good Catch Design
Edited by Peter Friend
Colour separations by
C.J.M. Graphics Pty. Ltd.
Printed and bound in China*

*The National Library of Australia
Cataloguing-in-Publication entry:
Duncan, Ken.
Sensational Sydney:
stunning panoramic views.
ISBN 0 9580544 1 X.
1. Sydney (N.S.W.) - Pictorial works.
2. Sydney (N.S.W.) - Description and
travel. I. title.
919.44100222*

*To view the range of Ken Duncan's
panoramic Limited Edition Prints
visit our Galleries situated at:-*
- *5740 Oak Road,
  Matcham, NSW
  Telephone +61 2 4367 6701*
- *73 George Street,
  The Rocks, Sydney, NSW
  Telephone +61 2 9241 3460*

- *Shop U6 Southgate,
  Melbourne, VIC
  Telephone +61 3 9686 8022*
- *Departures Level,
  Sydney International Airport,
  Mascot, NSW
  Telephone +61 2 9693 5355*